RECIPES FOR
MIXED DRINKS

BY
HUGO R. ENSSLIN

CONTENT

INTRODUCTION

The object of this book is to give a complete list of the standard mixed drinks that are in use at present in New York City, with directions for preparing same in the most simple manner to get the best result. It is intended for use in the home as well as a guide for those employed in Hotels, Clubs, etc.

For the benefit of those who are not familiar with the measures used by barkeepers, the following will be a help:

1 drink — ½ whiskey glass
1 jigger — ¼ whiskey glass
1 pony — 1 jigger

COCKTAILS

ABSINTHE COCKTAIL
¾ Absinthe
¼ Water
1 dash Gum Syrup
1 dash Angostura Bitters
Shake well in a mixing glass with cracked ice, strain and serve.

AFFINITY COCKTAIL
1/3 French Vermouth
1/3 Italian Vermouth
1/3 Scotch Whiskey
2 dashes Aromatic Bitters
Stir well in a mixing glass with cracked ice, strain and serve with a cherry and a twist of lemon peel over top of glass.

AFTER DINNER COCKTAIL (Special)
1 jigger Cederlund's Swedish Punch
½ jigger Cherry Cordial
Juice of ½ Lime
Shake well in a mixing glass with cracked ice, strain and serve in a Sherry glass.

AFTER DINNER COCKTAIL
½ Apricot Brandy
½ Curaçao
Juice of 1 Lime with rind
Shake well in a mixing glass with cracked ice, strain and serve.

ALEXANDER COCKTAIL
1/3 El Bart Gin
1/3 Crême de Cocoa
1/3 Sweet Cream
Shake well in a mixing glass with cracked ice, strain and serve.

ALICE COCKTAIL
½ Italian Vermouth
½ Russian Kummel
1 dash Scotch Whiskey
Shake well in a mixing glass with cracked ice, strain and serve.

APPETIZER No. I
½ Gin
½ Dubonnet
1 dash Scotch Whiskey
Shake well in a mixing glass with cracked ice, strain and serve.

APPETIZER No. II
1 drink of Dubonnet
Juice of ½ an Orange
Shake well in a mixing glass with cracked ice, strain and serve in a wine glass.

APPETIZER No. III
1 drink of Rye Whiskey
2 dashes of Peychaud Bitters
3 dashes Curaçao
Shake well in a mixing glass with cracked ice and a piece of lemon and orange peel, strain and serve.

APPETIZER No. IV
½ El Bart Gin
½ Dubonnet
1 dash Absinthe
Shake well in a mixing glass with cracked ice, strain and serve.

APPLE JACK COCKTAIL
1 drink of Apple Jack
2 dashes Gum Syrup
2 dashes Orange Bitters
1 dash Peychaud or Angostura Bitters
Stir well with cracked ice, strain and serve.

ATTENTION COCKTAIL
¼ French Vermouth
¼ Absinthe
¼ Gin
¼ Crême de Violette
Shake well in a mixing glass with cracked ice, strain and serve.

AVIATION COCKTAIL
1/3 Lemon Juice
2/3 El Bart Gin
2 dashes Maraschino
2 dashes Crême de Violette
Shake well in a mixing glass with cracked ice, strain and serve.

BARKING DOG
1/3 Italian Vermouth
1/3 French Vermouth
1/3 Gin
2 dashes Calisaya
Stir well in a mixing glass with cracked ice, strain and serve.

BAMBOO COCKTAIL
½ Sherry
½ Italian Vermouth
1 dash Angostura Bitters
Shake well with cracked ice, strain and serve.

BACARDI COCKTAIL
1 drink Bacardi Rum
Juice of ½ Lime
2 dashes Gum Syrup
Shake well in a mixing glass with cracked ice, strain and serve.

BARNEY FRENCH COCKTAIL

Use old fashioned cocktail glass.

Muddle well 4 slices of Orange
2 dashes Peychaud Bitters
1 piece Lemon Peel
Cube of Ice

Serve with Cascade Whiskey on the side.

BEAUTY SPOT

2/3 Gin
1/3 Grenadine
White of 1 Egg

Shake well in a mixing glass with cracked ice, strain and serve.

BELMONT COCKTAIL

2/3 Gin
1/3 Raspberry Syrup
Pony of sweet Cream

Shake well in a mixing glass with cracked ice, strain and serve.

BEST HOMEMADE

1 jigger of El Bart Gin
Juice of ½ an Orange

Shake well in a mixing glass with cracked ice, strain and serve.

BILL LYKENS DELIGHT

½ Dry Gin
½ Italian Vermouth
4 dashes Curaçao

Stir well in a mixing glass with cracked ice and a piece of orange
and lemon peel, strain and serve with a cherry.

BLACKTHORN

½ Italian Vermouth
½ Sloe Gin

Shake well in a mixing glass with cracked ice, strain and serve.

BLUE MOON COCKTAIL
2/3 Gin
1/3 French Vermouth
1 dash Orange Bitters
1 dash Crême Yvette
Stir well in a mixing glass with cracked ice, strain and top off with Claret.

BOLO COCKTAIL
1 Drink of Bacardi Rum
Juice of ½ Lime
Juice of ¼ of an Orange
1 bar spoonful Powdered Sugar
Shake well in a mixing glass with cracked ice, strain and serve.

BOBBY BURNS COCKTAIL
½ Italian Vermouth
½ Scotch Whiskey
2 dashes Benedictine
Stir well in a mixing glass with cracked ice, strain into cocktail glass and serve.

BOB DANBY COCKTAIL
1 jigger Dubonnet
½ jigger California Brandy
Shake well in a mixing glass with cracked ice, strain into cocktail glass and serve.

BONSONI COCKTAIL
1/3 Fernet Branca
2/3 Italian Vermouth
Shake well in a mixing glass with cracked ice, strain and serve.

BRAIN STORM COCKTAIL
Cube of Ice
2 dashes Benedictine
1 piece Orange Peel
2 dashes French Vermouth
1 drink of Irish Whiskey
Use an Old Fashioned Cocktail glass and serve with a small bar spoon in glass.

BRANDY COCKTAIL
1 jigger Brandy
2 dashes Gum Syrup
2 dashes Angostura Bitters
Shake well in a mixing glass with cracked ice, strain and serve.

BRONX COCKTAIL
½ Dry Gin
¼ French Vermouth
¼ Italian Vermouth
Juice of ¼ of an Orange
Shake well in a mixing glass with cracked ice, strain and serve.

BRONX (Dry)
3 slices Orange
1 slice Pineapple
½ Dry Gin
½ French Vermouth
Place fruit in mixing glass, muddle well, add cracked ice, gin and vermouth, shake well, strain into cocktail glass and serve.

GOLDEN BRONX COCKTAIL
Made same as Bronx adding the yolk of an egg.

SILVER BRONX COCKTAIL
or ORIENTAL COCKTAIL
Made same as Bronx adding white of an egg and a slice of Pineapple.

BULLDOG COCKTAIL
1 jigger Cherry Brandy
½ jigger Bacardi Rum
Juice ½ Lime

Shake well in a mixing glass with cracked ice, strain and serve in cocktail glass.

BUTTON HOOK COCKTAIL
¼ White Crême de Menthe
¼ Apricot Brandy
¼ Absinthe
¼ Brandy

Shake well in a mixing glass with cracked ice, strain and serve in a wine glass.

B.V.D. COCKTAIL
1/3 French Vermouth
1/3 El Bart Gin
1/3 Bacardi Rum

Stir well in a mixing glass with cracked ice, strain and serve.

CALISAYA COCKTAIL
½ Calisaya
½ Italian Vermouth
3 dashes Gum Syrup

Shake well in a mixing glass with cracked ice, strain and serve.

CANADIAN COCKTAIL
Juice of ½ Lemon
1 bar spoonful Powdered Sugar
1 pony Curaçao
3 dashes Jamaica Rum

Shake well in a mixing glass with cracked ice, strain and serve.

CASINO COCKTAIL
2 dashes Maraschino
2 dashes Orange Bitters

2 dashes Lemon Juice

1 drink of Tom Gin

Stir well in a mixing glass with cracked ice, strain and serve with a cherry.

CASTLE DIP COCKTAIL
½ Apple Brandy

½ White Crême de Menthe

3 dashes Absinthe

Shake well in a mixing glass with cracked ice, strain and serve.

CHOCOLATE COCKTAIL
1 teaspoonful Powdered Sugar

1 Egg

1 pony Maraschino

1 pony Chartreuse (yellow)

Shake well in a mixing glass with cracked ice, strain into a fancy glass and serve.

CARUSO COCKTAIL
1/3 French Vermouth

1/3 El Bart Gin

1/3 Crême de Menthe (green)

Stir well in a mixing glass with cracked ice, strain and serve.

CHAMPAGNE COCKTAIL
Use large Champagne goblet.

1 cube of Ice

1 dash Angostura Bitters

1 lump of Sugar

1 piece Orange Peel

1 piece Lemon Peel

Fill up with Champagne.

CHAPPELLE COCKTAIL
Muddle 3 slices Pineapple
1 jigger Italian Vermouth
1 jigger Dry Gin
Juice ½ Lime

Shake well in a mixing glass with cracked ice, strain and serve in cocktail glass.

CHRYSANTHEMUM COCKTAIL
3 dashes Absinthe
½ Benedictine
½ French Vermouth

Stir well in a mixing glass with cracked ice, strain and serve with a twist of Orange Peel.

CLUB COCKTAIL
2/3 Dry Gin
1/3 Italian Vermouth

Stir well in a mixing glass with cracked ice, strain and serve.

CLUB SODA COCKTAIL
Use long glass.

1 piece Loaf Sugar
2 dashes Angostura Bitters
Cube of Ice
1 piece Lemon Peel
1 bottle Club Soda

Stir in gently a small spoonful of Powdered Sugar and serve.

CLOVER LEAF COCKTAIL
1/3 Grenadine
2/3 Gin
White of an Egg
Juice of ½ Lime

Shake well in a mixing glass with cracked ice, strain and serve with a mint leaf on top.

CLOVER CLUB COCKTAIL
Made same as Clover Leaf Cocktail without the mint.

CREOLE COCKTAIL
½ Whiskey
½ Italian Vermouth
2 dashes Benedictine
2 dashes Amer-Picon
Stir well in a mixing glass with cracked ice, strain and serve with a twist of lemon peel on top.

CORONATION COCKTAIL
½ Sherry
½ French Vermouth
1 dash Maraschino
2 dashes Orange Bitters
Stir well in a mixing glass with cracked ice, strain and serve.

COOPERSTOWN COCKTAIL
1/3 El Bart Gin
1/3 French Vermouth
1/3 Italian Vermouth
Sprig fresh Mint
Shake well in a mixing glass with cracked ice, strain and serve.

CORNELL COCKTAIL
½ jigger Dry Gin
3 dashes Maraschino
1/3 Italian Vermouth
Sprig fresh Mint
Shake well in a mixing glass with cracked ice, strain and serve.

CUBAN COCKTAIL
1 jigger Bacardi Rum
2 dashes Gum Syrup
Juice of ½ Lime
Shake well in a mixing glass with cracked ice, strain and serve.

COFFEE COCKTAIL
1 Egg
1 bar spoonful Powdered Sugar
1 jigger Port Wine
½ jigger Brandy
Break egg into a mixing glass, add sugar, Port Wine, Brandy and cracked ice, shake well, strain and serve in Fifth Avenue glass.

CINCINNATI COCKTAIL
Half a glass of beer, fill up with soda water and serve.

DAIGUIRI COCKTAIL
1 jigger Bacardi Rum
2 dashes Grenadine Syrup
Juice of 1 Lime
Shake well in a mixing glass with cracked ice, strain and serve in a cocktail glass.

DUBONNET COCKTAIL
1 jigger Dubonnet
1 jigger Dry Gin
Stir well in a mixing glass with a cube of ice, strain and serve.

DEVIL'S COCKTAIL
½ Port Wine
½ French Vermouth
2 dashes Lemon Juice
Stir well in a mixing glass with cracked ice, strain and serve.

DIXIE COCKTAIL
½ jigger Dry Gin
¼ French Vermouth
¼ Absinthe
2 dashes Grenadine
Shake well in a mixing glass with cracked ice, strain and serve in a Sherry glass.

DICK JR., COCKTAIL
1/3 French Vermouth
1/3 Dry Gin
1/3 Apricot Brandy
Juice of 1 Lime
Shake well in a mixing glass with cracked ice, strain and serve.

DOCTOR COCKTAIL
1 jigger Cederlund's Punch
Juice 1 lime
Shake well in a mixing glass with cracked ice, strain into cocktail glass and serve very cold.

DRY COCKTAIL
1 jigger Hostetter Bitters
1 jigger Rye Whiskey
Stir well in a mixing glass with cracked ice, strain and serve with an olive in glass.

DUTCHESS COCKTAIL
1/3 French Vermouth
1/3 Italian Vermouth
1/3 Absinthe
Shake well in a mixing glass with cracked ice, strain and serve.

DUKE OF MARLBOROUGH COCKTAIL
½ Sherry Wine
½ Italian Vermouth
3 dashes Orange Bitters
Stir well in a mixing glass with cracked ice, strain and serve with a twist of orange peel on top.

DAVIS COCKTAIL
½ Jamaica Rum
½ French Vermouth
2 dashes Raspberry Syrup
Juice of 1 Lime
Shake well in a mixing glass with cracked ice, strain and serve.

DESHLER COCKTAIL
½ jigger Rye Whiskey
½ jigger Dubonnet
2 dashes Peychaud Bitters
2 dashes Contreau Triple Sec
1 piece Lemon Peel
2 pieces Orange Peel
Shake well in a mixing glass with cracked ice, strain and serve with a twist of orange peel on top.

ETHEL COCKTAIL
1/3 Apricot Brandy
1/3 Crême de Menthe (white)
½ jigger Curaçao (white)
Shake well in a mixing glass with cracked ice, strain and serve.

ELK COCKTAIL
½ Prunelle Brandy
2 dashes French Vermouth
½ El Bart Gin
Stir well in a mixing glass with cracked ice, strain and serve.

EVENDALE COCKTAIL
½ drink Evendale Special G
½ Pineapple or Orange Juice
Shake well in a mixing glass with cracked ice, strain and serve in cocktail glass.

EL BART BLOSSOM
1 drink El Bart Gin
Juice of ½ Blood Orange
Shake well in a mixing glass with cracked ice, strain and serve in a bar glass.

FOX TROT COCKTAIL
1 drink Bacardi Rum
2 dashes Curaçao
Juice of ½ Lime

Shake well in a mixing glass with cracked ice, strain and serve.

FIFTY FIFTY COCKTAIL
½ Dry Gin
½ French Vermouth
Stir well in a mixing glass with cracked ice, strain and serve.

FAIR AND WARMER COCKTAIL
1/3 Italian Vermouth
2/3 Bacardi Rum
2 dashes Curaçao
Stir well in a mixing glass with cracked ice, strain and serve with a twist of orange peel on top.

FLUFFY RUFFLES
½ Cuban Rum
½ Italian Vermouth
Rin of 1 Lime
Shake well in a mixing glass with cracked ice, strain and serve.

5:15 COCKTAIL
1/3 Curaçao
1/3 French Vermouth
1/3 Sweet Cream
Shake well in a mixing glass with cracked ice, strain and serve.

FLAG COCKTAIL
4 dashes Orange Curaçao, Triple Sec
½ pony Apricot Brandy
Shake well in a mixing glass with cracked ice, strain into a Sherry glass into the bottom of which is poured a spoonful of Crême Yvette and top with Claret.

GIN COCKTAIL
1 drink Dry Gin
1 dash Orange Bitters
Stir in a mixing glass with cracked ice, strain and serve with a twist of lemon peel.

GIBSON COCKTAIL
½ Gin
½ French Vermouth
Shake well in a mixing glass with cracked ice, strain and serve.

GOLF COCKTAIL (Dry)
1/3 French Vermouth
2/3 El Bart Gin
2 dashes Hostetter's Bitters
Stir well in a mixing glass with cracked ice, strain and serve with olive in glass.

HUGO BRACER
Juice of 1 Lime
2 dashes Grenadine syrup
1/3 Amer Picon
2/3 Apple Brandy
Shake well in a mixing glass with cracked ice and strain into a gobelet.

HUGO SPECIAL
6 slices Orange
3 slices Pineapple
1 jigger Gin
½ jigger Italian Vermouth
Place slices of orange and pineapple in a mixing glass and muddle well, add cracked ice, Gin and Vermouth, shake well, strain and serve in a stem glass.

HONOLULU COCKTAIL
1/3 Gin
1/3 Maraschino
1/3 Benedictine
Shake well in a mixing glass with cracked ice, strain and serve.

HARVARD
1 drink of Brandy
2 dashes Boker Bitters
Shake well in a mixing glass with cracked ice, strain and serve
with a twist of lemon peel on top.

HONEY MOON COCKTAIL
½ Benedictine
½ Apple Brandy
Juice of ½ lemon
3 dashes Curaçao
Shake well in a mixing glass with cracked ice, strain and serve.

"HAVE A HEART" COCKTAIL
½ jigger Cederlund's Swedish Punch
1 jigger Dry Gin
2 dashes Grenadine Syrup
Juice of ½ Lime
Shake well with fine ice, strain and serve in cocktail glass with
pineapple on edge and cherry atop pineapple.

HUMPTY DUMPTY COCKTAIL
1/3 Maraschino
2/3 French Vermouth
Shake well in a mixing glass with cracked ice, strain and serve.

IDEAL COCKTAIL
1/3 Italian Vermouth
2/3 Dry Gin
3 dashes of Maraschino
Juice of a small piece of grapefruit
Shake well in a mixing glass with cracked ice, strain and serve.

IMPERIAL COCKTAIL
½ French Vermouth
½ El Bart Gin
1 dash Angostura Bitters
1 dash of Maraschino

Stir well in a mixing glass with cracked ice, strain and serve with an olive.

ITALIAN COCKTAIL
2/3 Italian Vermouth
1/3 Fernet Branca
2 dashes Gum Syrup
1 dash Absinthe
Stir well in a mixing glass with cracked ice, strain and serve.

JACK ROSE
Juice and rind of 1 Lime
½ Apple Jack
½ Grenadine
Shake well in a mixing glass with cracked ice, strain and serve.

JACK SLOAT COCKTAIL
1 jigger El Bart Gin
2 dashes French Vermouth
4 dashes Italian Vermouth
3 slices of Pineapple
Juice of ¼ Orange
Shake well in a mixing glass with cracked ice, strain and serve.

JACKSON COCKTAIL
½ Orange Gin
½ Dubonnet
2 dashes Orange Bitters
Stir well in a mixing glass with cracked ice, strain and serve.

JAPANESE COCKTAIL
Use Old Fashioned Cocktail glass.
Cube of Ice
1 teaspoonful Orgeat Syrup
1 dash Angostura Bitters
1 drink of Brandy
Stir and serve with a spoon in glass and twist of lemon peel on top.

KING COLE COCKTAIL
Use Old Fashioned Cocktail glass.
1 jigger Boubon Whiskey
1 dash Fernet Branca
2 dashes Gum Syrup
1 slice of Orange
1 slice Pineapple

LONE TREE COCKTAIL
1/3 Italian Vermouth
1/3 French Vermouth
1/3 Dry Gin
2 dashes Orange Bitters
Shake well in a mixing glass with cracked ice, strain and serve.

LEAP FROG
Cube of Ice
Juice of ½ Lemon
1 jigger El Bart Gin
Split of Ginger Ale

Use Collins glass.

LA GRANDE FRANCE
½ Parfait d'Amour
½ Contreau, Triple Sec Curaçao
Serve in a cordial glass and top with cream and a cherry.

LOVE COCKTAIL
1 jigger Sloe Gin
White of 1 Egg
2 dashes Lemon Juice
2 dashes Raspberry Syrup
Shake well in a mixing glass with cracked ice, strain and serve.

LITTLE PRINCESS
½ Italian Vermouth
½ Cuban Rum
Shake well in a mixing glass with cracked ice, strain and serve.

LIEBFRAUMILCH COCKTAIL
1 jigger Creme de Cacao
1 jigger Cream
Juice of 1 Lime
Shake well in a mixing glass with cracked ice, strain and serve.

LITTLEST REBEL COCKTAIL
Juice of 1 Lime
1 jigger Apple Jack
½ jigger Scotch Whiskey
¼ jigger Grenadine
White of 1 Egg
Shake well in a mixing glass with cracked ice, strain and serve.

LADIES COCKTAIL
1 jigger Wilson Whiskey
2 dashes Absinthe
3 dashes Anisette
2 dashes Angostura Bitters
Stir well in a mixing glass with cracked ice, strain and serve with a piece of pineapple on top.

LONDON COCKTAIL
1 jigger Rye Whiskey
¼ jigger Orgeat Syrup
2 dashes Orange Flower Water
1 Egg
Shake well in a mixing glass with cracked ice, strain and serve with nutmeg on top.

LONDON SPECIAL
1 piece Domino Sugar
Peel of ½ Orange
Cube of Ice
2 dashes Peychaud Bitters
1 split imported Champagne
Use Champagne goblet.

LONDON BUCK
Cube of Ice
1 jigger Dry Gin
Juice of ½ Lemon
Split of Ginger Ale

Use Collins glass.

MARTINI COCKTAIL (DRY)
2/3 Dry Gin
1/3 French Vermouth
1 dash Orange Bitters

Stir well in a mixing glass with ice, strain and serve with olive in glass.

MARTINI COCKTAIL (SWEET)
2/3 Tom Gin
1/3 Italian Vermouth
2 dashes Gum Syrup
1 dash Orange Bitters

Stir well in a mixing glass with ice, strain and serve.

MABEL BERRA COCKTAIL
Juice of ½ Lime
½ jigger Swedish punch
½ jigger Sloe Gin

Shake well in a mixing glass with cracked ice, strain into a cocktail glass and serve.

MANHATTAN COCKTAIL (DRY)
2/3 Whiskey
1/3 Italian Vermouth
2 dashes Angostura Bitters

Stir well in a mixing glass with cracked ice, strain and serve with an olive in glass and a twist of lemon peel on top.

MANHATTAN COCKTAIL (SWEET)
Made same as Manhattan (dry) adding 2 dashes Gum Syrup and serve with a cherry instead of an olive.

MARY GARDEN
½ Dubonnet
½ French Vermouth
Stir well in a mixing glass with cracked ice, strain and serve.

MODERN COCKTAIL
1 drink Scotch Whiskey
2 dashes Lemon Juice
1 dash Absinthe
2 dashes Jamaica Rum
1 dash Orange Bitters
Shake well in a mixing glass with cracked ice, strain and serve with a cherry in glass.

MILLIONAIRE COCKTAIL I.
1/3 Jamaica Rum
1/3 Apricot Brandy
1/3 Sloe Gin
1 dash Grenadine
Juice of 1 Lime
Shake well in a mixing glass with cracked ice, strain and serve.

MILLIONAIRE COCKTAIL II.
2/3 Dry Gin
1/3 White Absinthe
White of 1 Egg
1 dash Anisette
Shake well in a mixing glass with cracked ice, strain and serve.

METROPOLITAN COCKTAIL
½ Brandy
½ Italian Vermouth
2 dashes Gum Syrup
1 dash Angostura Bitters
Shake well in a mixing glass with cracked ice, strain and serve.

MERRY WIDOW COCKTAIL
½ Dry Gin
½ French Vermouth
2 dashes Benedictine
1 dash Peychaud Bitters
2 dashes Absinthe

Stir well in a mixing glass with cracked ice, strain and serve with a twist of lemon peel on top.

MARGUERITE COCKTAIL
2/3 El Bart Gin
1/3 French Vermouth
1 dash Orange Bitters
1 piece Orange Peel

Shake well in a mixing glass with cracked ice, strain and serve.

MY COCKTAIL
1/3 Grand Marnier
2/3 Dry Gin

Shake well in a mixing glass with cracked ice, strain and serve.

MELBA COCKTAIL
½ jigger Bacardi Rum
2 dashes Absinthe
½ jigger Swedish Punch
Juice of ½ Lime
2 dashes Grenadine

Shake well in a mixing glass with cracked ice, strain and serve.

MOULIN ROUGE
½ Orange Gin
½ Apricot Brandy
3 dashes Grenadine

Stir well in a mixing glass with cracked ice, strain and serve.

MUD PIE
Use old fashioned Cocktail glass.
Muddle ½ piece Sugar and 2 dashes Peychaud Bitters
Cube of Ice
4 dashes Curaçao
Decorate with fruit and serve with whiskey on the side.

NOON COCKTAIL
Same as Bronx Cocktail adding white of an egg.

No. 6 COCKTAIL
1 jigger Dry Gin
½ jigger Italian Vermouth
1 piece Orange Peel
1 piece Lemon Peel
3 dashes Curaçao
Shake well in a mixing glass with cracked ice, strain and serve with a cherry in glass.

NEW YORK COCKTAIL
½ teaspoonful Powdered Sugar
1 jigger Rye Whiskey
Juice of 1 Lime or ½ Lemon
2 dashes Grenadine
1 piece Orange Peel
Shake well in a mixing glass with cracked ice, strain and serve with a twist of lemon peel on top.

ORANGE BLOSSOM COCKTAIL
1 drink Dry Gin
Juice of ½ Orange
Shake well in a mixing glass with cracked ice, strain and serve in a wine glass.

ONE OF MINE
Made same as a Bronx Cocktail, adding 1 dash Absinthe and 1 dash Hostetter

OPPENHEIM COCKTAIL
½ pony Bourbon
¼ pony Grenadine
¼ pony Italian Vermouth
Stir well in a mixing glass with cracked ice, strain and serve.

OLD FASHIONED APPETIZER
Use old fashioned Cocktail glass
Cube of Ice
½ jigger Rye or Bourbon
½ jigger Dubonnet
2 dashes Curaçao
2 dashes Absinthe
1 slice Orange
1 slice Pineapple
1 piece Lemon Peel
1 dash Peychaud Bitters
Serve with a small bar spoon in glass.

OLD FASHIONED COCKTAIL (GIN)
Use old fashioned Cocktail glass
½ piece Domino Sugar
2 dashes Angostura Bitters
1 drink El Bart Gin
1 slice Orange Peel
1 piece Lemon Peel
1 slice Pineapple
Muddle sugar and bitters, add cube of ice and the Gin, decorate with fruit.

OLD FASHIONED COCKTAIL (WHISKEY)
Made same as above, using Whiskey instead of Gin and 2 dashes Curaçao.

ORIENTAL COCKTAIL
See Silver Bronx.

ON THE WAY
½ Amer Picon
½ Italian Vermouth
Stir well in a mixing glass with cracked ice, strain and serve.

PALMER COCKTAIL
1 jigger Canadian Club Whiskey
1 dash Angostura Bitters
1 dash Lemon Juice
Shake well in a mixing glass with cracked ice, strain and serve.

POPPY COCKTAIL
1/3 Crême de Cacao
2/3 Dry Gin
Shake well in a mixing glass with cracked ice, strain and serve.

PICON COCKTAIL
½ Amer Picon
½ French Vermouth
Stir well with cracked ice, strain and serve.

PRESIDENT COCKTAIL
1 jigger Bacardi Rum
4 slices Orange
2 dashes Grenadine
Shake well in a mixing glass with cracked ice, strain and serve.

PERFECT COCKTAIL
1/3 French Vermouth
1/3 Italian Vermouth
1/3 Dry Gin
Shake well in a mixing glass with cracked ice, strain and serve.

POLLYANNA COCKTAIL
Muddle 3 slices Orange and 3 slices Pineapple
¼ pony Grenadine Syrup
1 jigger El Bart Gin
¼ jigger Italian Vermouth

Shake well in a mixing glass with cracked ice, strain into bar glass and serve.

PINKY COCKTAIL
½ Dry Gin
½ Grenadine
White of 1 Egg
Shake well in a mixing glass with cracked ice, strain and serve.

PERPETUAL COCKTAIL
½ Italian Vermouth
½ French Vermouth
2 dashes Crême de Cacao
4 dashes Crême Yvette
Shake well in a mixing glass with cracked ice, strain and serve.

PHOEBE SNOW
½ Dubonnet
½ Brandy
1 dash Absinthe
Shake well in a mixing glass with cracked ice, strain and serve.

PARADISE COCKTAIL
1/3 Apricot Brandy
1/3 El Bart Gin
1/3 Orange Juice
Shake well in a mixing glass with cracked ice, strain and serve.

PALMETTO COCKTAIL
½ St. Croix Rum
½ Italian Vermouth
2 dashes Orange Bitters
Stir well with cracked ice, strain and serve with a twist of lemon peel on top of glass.

POLO COCKTAIL
1/3 Italian Vermouth
1/3 French Vermouth

1/3 Dry Gin

Juice of ½ Lime

Shake well in a mixing glass with cracked ice, strain and serve.

PANAMA COCKTAIL
1/3 Dry Gin

1/3 Crême de Cacao

1/3 Sweet Cream

Shake well in a mixing glass with cracked ice, strain and serve.

PRINCETON COCKTAIL
2 dashes Lime Juice

1 jigger El Bart Gin

1 jigger French Vermouth

Shake well in a mixing glass with cracked ice, strain into cocktail glass and serve with an olive.

PRAIRIE HEN COCKTAIL
Use Old Fashioned Cocktail glass.

2 dashes Vinegar

1 Egg

1 dash each of Pepper and Salt

2 dashes Tabasco

1 teaspoonful Worcestershire Sauce

Serve with a little nutmeg on top.

QUEEN COCKTAIL
2/3 Dry Gin

1/3 Italian Vermouth

Muddle 3 slices Pineapple

Shake well in a mixing glass with cracked ice, strain and serve.

ROB ROY COCKTAIL
½ Scotch Whiskey

½ Italian Vermouth

2 dashes Gum Syrup

Shake well in a mixing glass with cracked ice, strain and serve.

ROYAL COCKTAIL
1 Egg
½ teaspoonful powdered sugar
Juice of ½ Lemon
1 jigger El Bart Gin
Shake well in a mixing glass with cracked ice, strain and serve in a Fifth Avenue glass.

RACQUET CLUB COCKTAIL
2/3 Plymouth Gin
1/3 French Vermouth
1 dash Orange Bitters
Shake well in a mixing glass with cracked ice, strain and serve.

RAYMOND HITCHCOCKTAIL
Juice of ½ Orange
1 drink Italian Vermouth
1 slice Pineapple
1 dash Orange Bitters
Shake well with cracked ice, strain and serve.

RAH-RAH-RUT
1 jigger Rye Whiskey
2 dashes Absinthe
2 dashes Peychaud Bitters
Shake well in a mixing glass with cracked ice, strain and serve.

RIDING CLUB COCKTAIL
½ wine glass Calisaya
3 dashes Horsford's Acid Phosphate
2 dashes Gum Syrup
Shake well in a mixing glass with cracked ice, strain and serve.

ROYAL SMILE COCKTAIL
½ Grenadine
2 dashes Lemon Juice
½ Dry Gin
Stir well with ice, strain and serve.

SANTIAGO COCKTAIL
1 jigger Bacardi Rum
Juice of 1 Lime
2 dashes Grenadine
Shake well in a mixing glass with cracked ice, strain and serve.

SOUTHERN GIN COCKTAIL
1 drink Dry Gin
2 dashes Orange Bitters
2 dashes Curaçao
Shake well in a mixing glass with cracked ice, strain and serve with a twist of lemon peel on top of glass.

SILVER KING COCKTAIL
White of 1 Egg
2 dashes Syrup
2 dashes Orange Bitters
Juice of ½ Lemon
1 jigger Gin
Shake well in a mixing glass with cracked ice, strain and serve.

SALOME COCKTAIL
1/3 French Vermouth
1/3 Dry Gin
1/3 Dubonnet
Shake well in a mixing glass with cracked ice, strain and serve.

SHRINER COCKTAIL
2 dashes Peychaud Bitters
2 dashes Gum Syrup
½ jigger Brandy
½ jigger Sloe Gin
Shake well in a mixing glass, strain into cocktail glass and serve with a twist of lemon peel on top.

SARATOGA COCKTAIL
1 jigger Brandy
2 dashes Pineapple Syrup

2 dashes Angostura Bitters
2 dashes Maraschino

Shake well in a mixing glass with cracked ice, strain into cocktail glass with a strawberry and a dash of carbonated water if desired.

SILVER COCKTAIL
½ French Vermouth
½ Holland Gin
1 dash Gum Syrup
2 dashes Orange Bitters
2 dashes Maraschino

Stir well in a mixing glass with cracked ice, strain and serve with a twist of lemon peel on top of glass.

SEPTEMBER MORN
1 jigger Bacardi Rum
Juice of ½ Lime
3 dashes Grenadine
White of 1 Egg

Shake well in a mixing glass with cracked ice, strain and serve.

SAXON COCKTAIL
Juice of ½ Lime
2 dashes Grenadine Syrup
1 jigger Bacardi Rum
1 piece of Orange Peel

Shake well in a mixing glass with cracked ice, strain and serve.

SNYDER COCKTAIL
2/3 Dry Gin
1/3 French Vermouth
2 dashes Curaçao

Stir well in a mixing glass with cracked ice, strain and serve in a large glass with a cube of ice and piece of orange peel.

STAR COCKTAIL
½ Applejack
½ Italian Vermouth
1 dash Gum Syrup
1 dash Angostura Bitters
Stir well with cracked ice, strain and serve.

SUBMARINE COCKTAIL
¼ French Vermouth
¼ El Bart Gin
½ Dubonnet
Stir well with cracked ice, strain into bar glass and serve.

SLOE GIN COCKTAIL
1 jigger Sloe Gin
1 dash Orange Bitters
1 dash French Vermouth
Stir well in a mixing glass with cracked ice, strain and serve.

SEVENTH REGIMENT COCKTAIL
½ Italian Vermouth
2/3 Dry Gin
2 pieces of Lemon Peel without the white
Shake well in a mixing glass with cracked ice, strain and serve.

SHAMROCK COCKTAIL
½ Irish Whiskey
½ French Vermouth
3 dashes Chartreuse (green)
3 dashes Crême de Menthe
Stir well with cracked ice, strain and serve with an olive in the glass.

STONEWALL JACKSON
1/3 Gin
1/3 Crême de Cacao
1/3 Sweet Cream
Shake well in a mixing glass with cracked ice, strain and serve.

SUNSHINE COCKTAIL
Juice of 1 Lime
2 dashes Crême de Cassis
½ Cuban Rum
½ French Vermouth
Shake well in a mixing glass with cracked ice, strain and serve.

SODA COCKTAIL
1 piece Domino Sugar
3 dashes Angostura Bitters
Large cube of Ice
1 piece Orange Peel
1 piece Lemon Peel
1 bottle Club or Lemon Soda
Use large Collins glass.
Stir in a large bar spoonful of powdered sugar and serve immediately.

SAZERAC COCKTAIL
Dissolve 1 lump of Sugar in a teaspoonful of water
1 dash Peychaud Bitters
1 jigger of Rye Whiskey
Stir well in a mixing glass with cracked ice, strain into another glass which has been cooled, add a dash of Absinthe and squeeze a piece of lemon peel on top.

SANGAREE COCKTAIL
Made same as Bronx Cocktail, adding ¼ pony Crême de Rose, 1 piece lemon peel and white of an egg.

TEMPTER COCKTAIL
½ Port Wine
½ Apricot Brandy
Shake well in a mixing glass with cracked ice, strain and serve in a wine glass.

TEMPTATION COCKTAIL
1 jigger Rye Whiskey

2 dashes Curaçao
2 dashes Absinthe
2 dashes Dubonnet
1 piece Orange Peel
1 piece Lemon Peel
Shake well in a mixing glass with cracked ice, strain and serve.

TIPPERARY COCKTAIL
1/3 Bushmills Irish Whiskey
1/3 Chartreuse
1/3 Italian Vermouth
Shake well in a mixing glass with cracked ice, strain and serve.

THREE STRIPES
2/3 Dry Gin
1/3 French Vermouth
3 slices Orange
Shake well in a mixing glass with cracked ice, strain and serve.

TINTON COCKTAIL
1/3 Port Wine
2/3 Applejack
Shake well in a mixing glass with cracked ice, strain and serve.

THIRD RAIL COCKTAIL
1 jigger French Vermouth
1 dash Curaçao
1 dash Essence of Mint
Stir well with cracked ice, strain and serve with a twist of orange peel.

TUXEDO COCKTAIL
1 drink Sherry Wine
½ pony Anisette
2 dashes Maraschino
1 dash Peychaud Bitters
Stir well with cracked ice, strain and serve.

TURF COCKTAIL
½ El Bart Gin
½ French Vermouth
2 dashes Absinthe
1 piece of Lemon Peel
Shake well in a mixing glass with cracked ice, strain and serve.

TRILBY COCKTAIL
½ El Bart Gin
½ Italian Vermouth
2 dashes Orange Bitters
Shake well in a mixing glass with cracked ice, strain into a cocktail glass, float a little Crême Yvette on top and serve.

UP TO DATE COCKTAIL
½ Sherry Wine
½ Rye Whiskey
2 dashes Angostura Bitters
2 dashes Grand Marnier
Shake well in a mixing glass with cracked ice, strain and serve.

UNION JACK COCKTAIL
1/3 Crême Yvette
2/3 Dry Gin
Shake well in a mixing glass with cracked ice, strain and serve.

VAN COCKTAIL
2/3 Dry Gin
1/3 French Vermouth
2 dashes Grand Marnier
Shake well in a mixing glass with cracked ice, strain and serve.

WALLICK COCKTAIL
½ French Vermouth
½ El Bert Gin
3 dashes Orange Flower Water
Shake well in a mixing glass with cracked ice, strain and serve.
Curaçao can be used if desired in place of Orange Flower Water.

WALLICK'S SPECIAL
1 jigger Brandy
½ Whiskey glass cream
White of 1 Egg
Juice of ½ Lime
½ teaspoonful powdered Sugar
2 dashes Grenadine
Shake well in a mixing glass with cracked ice, strain and serve.

WARD VIII
Made same as Dry Martini, adding 2 pieces orange peel.

WHITE WAY No. I.
1/3 White Crême de Menthe
2/3 Dry Gin
Shake well in a mixing glass with cracked ice, strain and serve.

WHITE WAY No. II.
1/3 Absinthe
1/3 Anisette
1/3 Brandy
Shake well in a mixing glass with cracked ice, strain and serve.

WELLINGTON COCKTAIL
Juice of ½ Lime
2 dashes Cherry Cordial
1 jigger dry Gin
2 dashes Swedish Punch
Shake well in a mixing glass with cracked ice, strain into a cocktail glass and serve.

WHITE ROSE COCKTAIL
1 jigger El Bart Gin
Juice of ¼ Orange
Juice of 1 Lime
½ jigger Maraschino
White of 1 Egg

Shake well in a mixing glass with cracked ice, strain and serve in a wine glass.

WIDOW'S DREAM COCKTAIL
1 drink Benedictine
1 cold fresh EGG
Fill up with Cream

Use Cocktail glass.

YACHTING CLUB COCKTAIL
2/3 Holland Gin
1/3 French Vermouth
2 dashes Gum Syrup
2 dashes Peychaud Bitters
1 dash Absinthe

Shake well in a mixing glass with cracked ice, strain and serve.

YALE COCKTAIL
3 dashes Orange Bitters
2 dashes Gum Syrup
1 dash Maraschino
½ jigger French Vermouth
1 jigger Dry Gin

Stir well in a mixing glass with cracked ice, strain into cocktail glass and serve.

ZAZA COCKTAIL
1 jigger Dry Gin
1 jigger Dubonnet
1 piece Orange Peel

Shake well in a mixing glass with cracked ice, strain and serve.

COOLERS

APRICOT COOLER
Juice of ½ Lemon
Juice of ½ Lime
2 dashes Grenadine Syrup
½ drink Apricot Brandy
Shake in a mixing glass with cracked ice, strain into a Collins glass, add a cube of ice and fill up with Club Soda.

HARVARD COOLER
1 pony Sugar Syrup
Juice of ½ Lemon or 1 Lime
1 jigger Applejack
Made and served same as Apricot Cooler.

MANHATTAN COOLER
Juice of 1 Lime
½ spoonful Powdered Sugar
1 wine glass of Claret
3 dashes ST. Croix Rum
Stir well in a mixing glass with cracked ice, pour into a stem glass, decorate with fruit and serve with straws.

LONG TOM COOLER
1 pony Sugar Syrup
Juice of ½ Lemon
1 drink El Bart Gin
Shake well in a mixing glass with cracked ice, strain into a Collins glass, add a cube of ice and 1 slice of Orange, fill up with Club Soda.

LONE TREE COOLER
Juice of 1 Lemon
Juice ¼ Orange
1 pony Grenadine
Made and served same as Apricot Cooler.

RAIL SPLITTER
1 pony Syrup
Juice ½ Lemon
Shake well in a mixing glass with cracked ice, strain into a Collins glass, add a cube of ice and fill up with Ginger Beer.

REMSEN COOLER
1 drink Dry Gin or Scotch Whiskey
1 Lemon
1 bottle Club Soda
Peel off rind of lemon in spiral form, place in Collins glass with cube of ice, add Gin or Scotch and fill up with Club Soda.

STONE FENCE
Use Collins glass.
1 cube of Ice
2 dashes Peychaud Bitters
1 drink Scotch Whiskey
Fill up with Carbonated Water or Club Soda.

SARAGOTA COOLER
Use Collins glass.
Juice of ½ Lemon
½ teaspoonful Powdered Sugar
2 dashes Angostura Bitters
1 bottle Ginger Ale (cold)
Stir slowly and serve.

SCOTCH COOLER
1 cube of Ice
1 drink Scotch Whiskey
3 dashes Crême de Menthe
Split of Club Soda or Carbonated Water
Use Collins glass.

CUPS

BURGUNDY CUP (10 persons)
1 whiskey glass Brandy
½ whiskey glass Curaçao
½ whiskey glass Benedictine
1 ½ quarts Burgundy
1 pint sparkling Mineral Water
4 tablespoonsful powdered Sugar
Mix and serve same as Champagne Cup.

CHAMPAGNE CUP
1 drink Brandy
2 tablespoons Powdered Sugar or ½ glass Syrup
½ jigger Curaçao
¼ jigger Maraschino
¼ Grand Marnier
1 qt. imported or domestic Champagne
Serve in a large glass pitcher with squares of ice, decorate with slices of Orange and Pineapple, Cherries and 1 slice of Cucumber peel. Bunch of fresh Mint on top. Serve a long spoon with the cup and stem glasses.

CLARET CUP
¼ jigger Maraschino
½ jigger Curaçao
3 tablespoons Powdered Sugar or 1 bar glass of Syrup
1 qt. Claret or Burgundy
Serve same as Champagne Cup.

RHINE WINE CUP
½ jigger Maraschino
¼ jigger Curaçao
¼ jigger Syrup
1 qt. Rhine Wine
Serve same as Champagne Cup.

SAUTERNE CUP

Made and served same as Rhine Wine Cup, using Sauterne in place of Rhine Wine.

TEMPERENCE CUP

Juice of 4 Oranges
Juice of 1 Lemon
Juice of 5 Limes
3 tablespoonsful Powdered Sugar
1 qt. Grape Juice (Red or White)

Serve same as Champagne Cup.

DAISIES

BRANDY DAISY
GIN DAISY
RUM DAISY
WHISKEY DAISY

All the above Daisies are made as follows:

Juice ½ Lime and ¼ Lemon
1 teaspoonful Powdered Sugar
2 dashes Grenadine
1 drink of liquor desired
2 dashes Carbonated Water

Use silver mug, put in above ingredients, fill up with fine ice, stir until mug is frosted, decorate with fruit and sprays of fresh mint and serve with straws.

FIZZES

ALABAMA FIZZ

Made same as Gin Fizz, adding a sprig of fresh Mint.

APPLE BLOW FIZZ

1 drink Applejack
4 dashes Lemon Juice
1 spoonful Sugar
White of 1 Egg

Shake well in a mixing glass with cracked ice, strain into a fizz glass, fill up with carbonated or any sparkling water desired.

ALBEMARLE FIZZ

Made same as plain Gin Fizz, adding Raspberry Syrup.

BRANDY FIZZ
Made same as plain Gin Fizz, using Brandy instead of Gin.

BOOT LEG
Made same as Silver Fizz, adding sprigs of Mint.

DERBY FIZZ
1 jigger Whiskey
5 dashes Lemon Juice
1 teaspoonful Sugar
1 Egg (white and yolk)
3 dashes Curaçao

Shake well in a mixing glass with cracked ice, strain into a fizz glass, fill up with carbonated or any sparkling water desired.

GIN FIZZ
Juice of ½ Lime
Juice ½ Lemon
1 tablespoonful Powdered Sugar
1 drink Dry Gin

Shake well in a mixing glass with cracked ice, strain into a fizz glass, fill up with carbonated or any sparkling water desired.

GOLDEN FIZZ
Made same as plain Gin Fizz, adding the yolk of an egg.

GRAND ROYAL FIZZ
Made same as plain Gin Fizz, adding
1 dash Maraschino
3 dashes Orange Juice
½ pony Cream

IMPERIAL FIZZ
1/3 St. Croix Rum
2/3 Whiskey
4 dashes Lemon Juice
Juice ½ Lime

Shake well in a mixing glass with cracked ice, strain into a fizz glass, fill up with carbonated or any sparkling water desired.

MORNING GLORY FIZZ
Juice of ½ Lime
Juice ½ Lemon
1 teaspoonful Powdered Sugar
White of 1 Egg
2 dashes Absinthe
1 drink Scotch Whiskey
Made and served as directed for plain Gin Fizz.

NEW ORLEANS FIZZ
Juice of ½ Lime
Juice ½ Lemon
2 teaspoonful Powdered Sugar
White of 1 Egg
1 drink Gin
3 dashes Orange Flower Water
½ pony Cream
Made and served as directed for plain Gin Fizz.

ORANGE FIZZ
Juice ½ Orange
Juice ½ Lime
Juice ½ Lemon
Drink El Bart Gin
Made and served as directed for plain Gin Fizz.

ROYAL FIZZ
Made same as plain Gin Fizz, adding the whole of one egg.

PEACH BLOW FIZZ
Juice ½ Lime
Juice ½ Lemon
4 Strawberries, mashed up
1 teaspoonful Powdered Sugar

1 drink Gin
1 pony Cream
Made and served as directed for plain Gin Fizz.

RUBY FIZZ
Juice ½ Lemon
1 teaspoonful Powdered Sugar
White 1 Egg
2 dashes Raspberry Syrup
1 drink Sloe Gin
Shake and serve as directed for Gin Fizz.

ROSE IN JUNE
Juice 1 Orange
Juice 2 Limes
1 jigger Raspberry Syrup
1 jigger Gin
Shake well in a mixing glass with cracked ice, strain into Collins glass and fizz with sparkling water.

SILVER BALL
Juice ¼ Grapefruit
White of an egg
1 teaspoonful powdered Sugar
2 dashes Orange Flower Water
1 drink Rhine Wine
Shake well in a mixing glass with cracked ice, strain into Collins glass and fizz with siphon of carbonated water.

SILVER FIZZ
Made same as plain Gin Fizz, adding the white of an egg.

SLOE GIN FIZZ
Made same as plain Gin Fizz, using Sloe Gin instead of Dry Gin.

ST. CROIX RUM FIZZ
Made same as plain Gin Fizz, using St Croix Rum instead of Gin.

SOUTH SIDE FIZZ
Made same as Gin Fizz, adding fresh mint leaves.

FLIPS

BLACKBERRY FLIP
BRANDY FLIP
CHERRY BRANDY FLIP
PORT WINE FLIP
RUM FLIP
WHISKEY FLIP

All the above Flips are made as follows:

1 Egg

1 teaspoonful Powdered Sugar

1 drink of liquor desired

Shake well in a mixing glass with cracked ice, strain and serve in a stem glass with Nutmeg on top.

BRANDY GINGER FLIP
Made same as Brandy Flip, adding two dashes Jamaica Ginger.

WHISKEY PEPPERMINT FLIP
Made same as Whiskey Flip, adding ¼ pony of essence of Peppermint

HIGHBALLS

RYE HIGHBALL
BOURBON HIGHBALL
SCOTCH HIGHBALL
IRISH HIGHBALL
GIN HIGHBALL
GRAPE JUICE HIGHBALL
RUM HIGHBALL
DUBONNET HIGHBALL
MINT HIGHBALL
BITTERS HIGHBALL
CORDIALS HIGHBALL

All the above Flips are made as follows:
Use highball glass with cube of ice, add one drink of liquor desired, fill up with carbonated water or Ginger Ale. Serve with
small bar spoon in glass and a piece of lemon peel if desired.

PICON HIGHBALL
1 Drink of Amer Picon
3 dashes Grenadine or Curaçao
Serve same as other Highballs.

CEDERLUND'S SWEDISH PUNCH HIGHBALL
1 drink Cederlund's Swedish Punch
1 dash bitters
Place a cube of ice in highball glass, add the Swedisg punch and
bitters and fill up with Club Soda or other carbonated water.

HOT DRINKS

APPLE TODDY
Use hot water glass.

2 pieces Domino Sugar
¼ Baked Apple
1 drink Apple Brandy

Fill up with hot water, stir and serve. Put a little Nutmeg on top if desired.

HOT GIN
Use hot water glass.

Juice of 1 Lemon
2 pieces Domino Sugar
1 drink of Gin

Fill up with hot water and serve with a spoon.

HOT LEMONADE
Use hot water glass.

Juice of 1 Lemon
2 pieces Domino Sugar

Fill glass up with hot water, stir and serve with a spoon.

HOT RUM
Use hot water glass.

1 piece Domino Sugar dissolved in a little hot water
1 drink Jamaica Rum

Fill up with hot water and serve with a twist of Lemon Peel.

HOT SPICED RUM
Made same as Hot Rum, adding a few cloves and allspice. If desired add small piece of butter.

HOT WHISKEY

Use hot water glass.

Dissolve 1 piece Domino Sugar in a little hot water, add 1 piece cinnamon and 1 piece of lemon peel and cloves, 1 drink of whiskey desired. Serve hot water separate in a silver pitcher. Add small piece of butter if desired.

HOT SCOTCH

Made same as Hot Whiskey, using Scotch Whiskey instead of Rye.

TOM AND JERRY

1 Egg
½ jigger Jamaica Rum
1 teaspoonful Powdered Sugar
¼ teaspoonful Powdered Allspice
¼ pony Brandy

Mix well together the yolk of the egg, Jamaica Rum, Sugar and Allspice, then add the white of the egg beaten to a stiff froth, and the Brandy. Serve in a silver mug with hot water or hot milk as desired and top with Nutmeg.

LEMONADES

PLAIN LEMONADE
½ Lemon
½ Lime
2 tablespoonsful Powdered Sugar
Muddle well in a mixing glass, add fine ice and still spring or filtered water, shake well, strain into a Collins glass, add some cracked ice, decorate with slices of Orange, Pineapple and some cherries and serve with straws.

ASTOR LEMONADE
Made same as Plain Lemonade, adding 1 pony Grenadine in the bottom of the serving glass.

CALIFORNIA LEMONADE
Juice of 1 Lemon
Juice of 1 Lime
1 tablespoonful Powdered Sugar
1 jigger Rye Whiskey
1 dash Grenadine
Shake well in a mixing glass with cracked ice, strain into Collins glass and fill up with carbonated or any sparkling water.

CLARET LEMONADE
Made same as Plain Lemonade, adding Claret on top.

LEMONADE D'ORGEAT
½ teaspoonful powdered Sugar
Juice 1 Lemon
½ bar glass Orgeat Syrup
Shake well in a mixing glass with cracked ice and filtered or still spring water, pour into Collins glass, add more ice if necessary, decorate with fruit and serve with straws.

EGG LEMONADE

Made same as Plain Lemonade, adding Claret on top.

FRUIT LEMONADE
Made same as Plain Lemonade, with plenty of fruit and a pony glass of Raspberry Syrup in bottom of serving glass.

GOLDEN LEMONADE
Juice of 2 Limes
1 tablespoonful Powdered Sugar
Yolk of 1 Egg
1 pony Amer Picon
1 pony Eau de Vie de Dantzig
Shake well in a mixing glass with cracked ice, strain into a Collins glass and fill up with carbonated or any sparkling water.

MODERN LEMONADE
1 Lemon
2 tablespoonsful Powdered Sugar
1 pony Sherry
1 pony Sloe Gin
Cut lemon in quarters and muddle well with the sugar, put into mixing glass with cracked ice, add the Sherry and Sloe Gin, shake well, strain into a Collins glass and fill up with carbonated or any sparkling water.

PINEAPPLE LEMONADE
2 slices Pineapple
1 dash Raspberry Syrup
1 jigger Brandy
1 teaspoonful Powdered Sugar
Muddle the pineapple and sugar well, put into mixing glass, add cracked ice and the Brandy and Raspberry Syrup, shake well, pour into Collins glass, fill up with carbonated or any sparkling water, decorate with a slice of pineapple and serve with straws.

SELTZER LEMONADE
Made same as Plain Lemonade, using carbonated water, only dont shake the mixture, stir it.

LIMEADE
Juice of 3 Limes

2 tablespoonsful Powdered Sugar

Shake well in a mixing glass with cracked ice and filtered or still
spring water, pour into Collins glass, decorate with fruit and serve
with straws.

SOUTHERN MINT JULEP
Use Collins glass.

6 sprigs of fresh Mint

1 tablespoonful Powdered Sugar

1 drink Rye or Bourbon

Muddle gently the mint and sugar, add the Rye or Bourbon, fill up
with fine ice, stir gently until glass is frosted, decorate with fresh
mint and serve with straws. Top off with Jamaica Rum if desired.

PUNCHES

AMERICAN PUNCH
Use Collins glass.

1 tablespoonful Powdered Sugar
Juice of 1 Lemon
1 dash Grenadine
½ drink Crême de Menthe (white)
½ drink Crême de Yvette

Place sugar and lemon juice in bottom of glass and dissolve with carbonated water (small quantity) fill up with cracked ice, float cordials on top, keeping each separate as in pousse café, and decorate with fruit.

BACARDI RUM PUNCH
Use Collins glass.

1 jigger Gum Syrup or Grenadine
1 drink Bacardi Rum

Place syrup or Grenadine in glass, fill up with fine ice, add Rum, stir until glass is frosted, decorate with fruit and serve with straws.

BRANDY PUNCH (Two gallons)
Juice of 15 Lemons
Juice of 4 Oranges
1 ¼ lb. Powdered Sugar
½ pint Curaçao
1 bar glass of Raspberry or Grenadine Syrup
2 quarts Brandy

Place large block of ice in a punch bowl, add above ingredients and from one to two quarts of sparkling mineral water as desired. Serve in punch glasses.

BOMBAY PUNCH (Two gallons)
1 qt. of Brandy
1 qt. Sherry

¼ pt. Maraschino
½ pt. Orange Curaçao
4 qts. Champagne
2 qts. Carbonated Water

Stir the above gently. Surround a punch bowl up to the top with cracked ice and decorate the edge with fruits—grapes, oranges, pineapple, etc., pour punch into bowl and when cool serve in small punch glasses. Never put ice into the punch.

CARDINAL PUNCH

1 ½ pounds Domino Sugar
2 qts. sparkling Mineral Water
2 qts. Claret
1 pt. Brandy
1 pt. Rum
1 pt. sparkling White Wine
1 bar glass of Italian Vermouth
Sliced Oranges and Pineapple

Place sugar in bottom of bowl and dissolve with Mineral Water put in a bock of ice and the above ingredients.

CLARET PUNCH

½ lb. Powdered Sugar
3 qts. Claret
2 qts. Sparkling Water
½ pt. Lemon Juice
1 Whiskey glass Curacao

Mix well, pour into punch bowl, surround bowl with cracked ice. Cut up oranges and pineapple and add some cherries, place in a separate bowl and serve in the glasses with the punch. The above is sufficient for ten persons. If more punch is desired, increase quantities in proportion.

CHAMPAGNE PUNCH

½ lb. Powdered Sugar
2 qts. Champagne (imported or domestic)

1 qt. Mineral Water
1 Whiskey glass Brandy
1 Whiskey glass Maraschino
1 Whiskey glass Curaçao

Mix well, pour into punch bowl, surround bowl with cracked ice and add cut fruit.

FISH HOUSE PUNCH
Juice of 6 lemons
½ lb. Powdered Sugar
½ pt. Brandy
¼ pt. Peach Brandy
¼ pt. Jamaica Rum
3 qts. Sparkling Water

Place a large block of ice in a punch bowl, add the above ingredients. Serve when cool in punch glasses.

GIN PUNCH
Use Collins glass.
1 piece Domino Sugar
1 piece Lemon Peel
Juice of ½ Lemon
1 Jigger Dry Gin
2 dashes Maraschino

Add some cracked ice, fill up with sparkling water and serve with a long spoon in a glass.

LADIES PUNCH
2 teaspoonsful Powdered Sugar
1 Egg
½ pony Maraschino
1 pony Crême de Cacao
1 piece Orange Peel
2 dashes Nutmeg
1 glass Milk

Shake well in a mixing glass with cracked ice, strain into Collins glass, serve with Nutmeg on top.

MAY WINE (sufficient for ten persons)
5 bunches Woodruff (Waldmeister)
½ lb. Powdered Sugar
½ pt. Brandy
1 qt. White Wine

Let the above stand five hours and strain through cheese cloth, add:

3 qts. White Wine
1 qt. Sparkling Water
1 qt. Champagne (imported or domestic).

Pour above mixture into bowl, surround bowl with cracked ice, add cut up fruit and serve.

PINEAPPLE PUNCH (10 persons)
½ whiskey glass Pineapple syrup
½ whiskey glass Grenadine Syrup
½ whiskey glass Maraschino
1 whiskey glass Sweet Gin
Juice 3 Lemons
5 dashed Aromatic Bitters
1 ½ quarts Moselle Wine
1 quart sparkling water

Mix well, pour into Punch bowl, surround bowl with cracked ice, and add one ripe pineapple cut in small cubes.

PANAMA PUNCH

Use Collins glass.

Juice of 1 lime
1 teaspoonful Powdered Sugar
1 drink Jamaica Rum

Place Lime Juice and Sugar in bottom of glass and dissolve with carbonated water (small quantity), fill up with fine ice, fizz with carbonated water and serve with straws.

REGENT PUNCH (10 persons)

1 whiskey glass Cognac
1 whiskey glass Swedish punch
½ whiskey glass Curacao
1 pint Jamaica Rum
Juice 6 Lemons
1 ½ quarts Champagne
1 teaspoonful Aromatic Bitter
2 tablespoonful good Tea

Put tea in a small cheese cloth bag and leave in the above mixture for about ten minutes, surround punch bowl with cracked ice, pour in the punch and add cut up fruit.

ROMAN PUNCH

1 qt. Champagne
1 qt. Rum
½ jigger Orange Bitters
Juice of 10 Lemons
Juice of 3 Oranges
2 lbs. Sugar
10 Eggs, whites only

Dissolve sugar in lemon and orange juice with the rind of one orange, strain into punch bowl, add the beaten whites of the eggs. Surround bowl with cracked ice, when thoroughly chilled stir in Rum and Champagne and mix well.

MILK PUNCHES
Rye Milk Punch
Scotch Milk Punch
Bourbon Milk Punch
Jamaica Rum Milk Punch
Applejack Milk Punch
Grenadine Milk Punch
Brandy Milk Punch
Bacardi Rum Milk Punch
Any other liquor with milk

All the above Milk Punches are made as follows:
One glass sweet milk, tablespoonful of powdered sugar and one drink of liquor desired. Shake well in a mixing glass with cracked ice for about three minutes, strain into large glass and serve with Nutmeg or a piece of Lemon or Orange peel on top.

MILK PUNCH (HOT)
Prepare this punch same as cold Milk Punch, using hot milk and no ice.

MILK SHAKE
1 tablespoonful Sugar
1 Egg
1 glass of sweet Milk

Shake well in a mixing glass with cracked ice, strain into stem glass and serve with Nutmeg on top.

RHINE WINE PUNCH (sufficient for ten persons)
½ lb. Powdered Sugar
3 qts. Rhine Wine
1 qt. Sparkling Mineral Water
1 Whiskey glass Brandy
1 Whiskey glass Maraschino
2 tablespoonsful of good Tea

Put tea in a small cheese cloth bag and leave in the above mixture for about ten minutes, surround a punch bowl with cracked ice, pour in punch and add cut up fruit.

ST CROIX RUM PUNCH
Use Collins glass.

Juice of 1 Lemon
1 tablespoonful of Sugar, dissolved in a little water
½ wine glass of St. Croix Rum

Fill glass up with fine ice, decorate with fruit and serve with straws.

STRAWBERRY PUNCH
12 Strawberries, mashed up
1 pony Brandy
2 teaspoonsful Powdered Sugar
1 glass fresh Milk

Shake well with cracked ice, strain into a Collins glass and serve with a twist of orange peel on top.

SAUTERNE PUNCH
½ lb. Powdered Sugar
2 qts. Sauterne, domestic or imported
1 Whiskey glass Maraschino
1 Whiskey glass Curacao
1 Whiskey glass Grand Marnier

Place a large block of ice in a punch bowl, add the above mixture with some cut up fruit and serve.

THE BEST PUNCH
1 cup strong Tea
Juice of 2 Lemons
1 teaspoonful Sugar
½ wine glass Brandy
1 pony Curacao

1 pony Medford Rum

1 qt. Champagne

Place a large block of ice in punch bowl, add the above mixture and one quart of sparkling water. More water can be used if desired.

TEMPERANCE PUNCH N°1

½ lb. Powdered Sugar

2 qts. cold Tea

1 pt. Lemon Juice

1 1 qt. Sparkling Mineral Water

1 qt. White Grape Juice

Place large block of ice in punch bowl, pour in the punch and add some cut up fruit.

TEMPERANCE PUNCH N°2

½ lb. Powdered Sugar

½ pt. Lemon Juice

1 qt. Mineral Water

2 qts. Red Grape Juice

Place large block of ice in punch bowl, pour in the punch and add some cut up fruit.

RICKEYS

Gin Rickey	Grenadine Rickey
Rye Rickey	Applejack Rickey
Bourbon Rickey	Rum Rickey
Scotch Rickey	Amer Picon Rickey
Irish Rickey	Sloe Gin Rickey
Apricot Rickey	Raspberry Rickey

Cordials (any kind) Rickey

All the above Rickeys are made as follows:
Use highball glass with cube of ice, juice of ½ or whole Lime, 1 drink of liquor desired. Fill up with carbonated water and serve with small bar spoon in glass.

PORTO RICO RICKEY
Made same as Gin Rickey, adding 2 dashes Raspberry Syrup.

HUGO RICKEY
Made same as Gin Rickey, adding 2 dashes Grenadine and 1 slice of pineapple.

SMASHES

BRANDY SMASH
GIN SMASH
RUM SMASH
SCOTCH SMASH
WHISKEY (RYE OR BOURBON)

All the above Smashes are made as follows:

Use Old Fashioned Cocktail glass.

Dissolve ½ piece Domino Sugar in a little carbonated water, add four sprigs of fresh Mint and muddle slightly. Place a cube of ice in the glass, add one drink of liquor desired and serve with a sprig of Mint on top.

SOURS

APPLEJACK SOUR
1 drink Applejack
Juice of ½ Lime
Juice of ½ Lemon
1 dash Grenadine
1 teaspoonful Powdered Sugar

Shake well in a mixing glass with cracked ice, strain into a Fifth Avenue glass, decorate with fruit and serve. Fill up with carbonated water if desired.

BRANDY SOUR

Made same as Whiskey Sour using Brandy instead of Whiskey.

FIREMAN'S SOUR
½ pony Grenadine
½ teaspoonful Powdered Sugar
1 drink Bacardi Rum
Juice of 1 Lime
Made and served same as Applejack Sour.

GIN SOUR
Made same as Whiskey Sour using Gin instead of Whiskey.

JAMAICA RUM SOUR
Made same as St. Croix using Jamaica Rum instead of St. Croix.

ST. CROIX RUM SOUR
Juice of ½ Lemon
Juice ½ Lime
1 pony Gum Syrup
1 jigger St. Croix Rum
Made and served same as Applejack Sour.

WHISKEY SOUR
1 teaspoonful Powdered Sugar
Juice of ½ Lime
Juice of ½ Lemon
Shake well in a mixing glass with cracked ice, strain into a stem glass and decorate with fruit. If desired fizz with carbonated water.

MISCELLANEOUS MIXED DRINKS

APPLE PIE
Plain Lemonade with one drink of Scotch Whiskey.

ANGEL'S WINGS
Use Cordial Glass
1/3 Raspberry
1/3 Maraschino
1/3 Crême de Violette
Top with Cream and decorate with a cherry.

ANGEL'S KISS
Use Cordial Glass
½ Crême Yvette
½ Benedictine
Cream top

ABSINTHE FRAPPE
1 jigger Green Absinthe
3 dashes Gum Syrup or Anisette
Shake well in a mixing glass with cracked ice, strain and serve in a Delmonico Glass. If desired fill up with carbonated water.

ABSINTHE DRIP
Use Absinthe Drip glass.
Put 1 pony of green or white Absinthe in the bowl, fill top of glass with fine ice, add 1 piece of Domino Sugar, pour in a ½ pint of water and serve.

AFTER DINNER SPECIAL
½ Apricot Brandy
½ Curacao
Juice and rind of 1 Lime

Shake well in mixing glass with cracked ice, strain into a cocktail glass and serve.

AFTER DINNER PUNCH
This made the same as After Dinner Special, only the mixture is left in the ice, served in a Fifth Avenue glass and decorated with fruit.

BRANDY TODDY
Use Old Fashioned Cocktail Glass.

Muddle a ½ piece of Domino Sugar in a little carbonated water, add cube of ice. Serve bottle of Brandy desired, so customer may help himself.

BRANDY BLASER
Use a small bowl.

2 pieces Domino Sugar
1 drink Brandy
1 piece of Orange Peel
1 piece Lemon Peel

Light with a match, stir with a long spoon for a few seconds, pour into bar glass and serve.

BRANDY FLOAT
Use Fifth Avenue Glass.

Fill ¾ full of carbonated water and float a pony of Brandy on top.

BABY'S OWN
Use Cordial Glass
2/3 White Curaçao
1/3 Cream
1 drop Angostura Bitters

BUCK AND BREAK
Use Collins glass.
Moisten glass with Lime or Lemon Juice
Frost with powdered sugar
1 cube of ice
1 pony Brandy
Fill up with Champagne

TOM COLLINS
1 tablespoonful Powdered sugar
Juice of 1 Lemon or 2 Limes
1 drink any Gin desired
Shake well in a mixing glass with cracked ice, strain into a Collin glass, add a cube of ice and a bottle of Club Soda, stir and serve.

JOHN COLLINS
Same as Toms Collins, using Holland Gin.

CHAMPAGNE COBBLER
Use Collins glass.
Fill 1/3 with fine ice, and 1 teaspoonful powdered sugar, 1 piece of Orange peel, fill up with split of Champagne desired and decorate with fruit.

CHAMPAGNE VELVET
Use Stem glass.
Fill glass half with Stout, which must be cold, and fill up

with Champagne desired. Pour very slowly or glass will overflow.

CLARET COBBLER
Made same as Champagne Cobbler, using Claret instead of Champagne.

DOUBLE ARROW HEAD
Use Cordial glass.

½ White Curaçao
½ Crême Yvette
Cream top

EGG PHOSPHATE
1 Egg
1 teaspoonful Powdered Sugar
1 teaspoonful Acid Phosphate

Shake well in a mixing glass with cracked ice, strain into a Collins glass and fill up with carbonated water

EGG NOGG
1 Egg
1 teaspoonful Powdered Sugar
1 drink Jamaica Rum or Brandy
¾ glass Milk

Shake well in a mixing glass with cracked ice, strain into a Collins glass and serve with Nutmeg on top.

FLORIDA SPECIAL
Use Collins glass.

1 cube of Ice
Juice of ½ Orange
Rind of 1 Orange

Peel Orange rind in spiral form and place in glass with Orange juice and ice and fill up with Ginger Ale.

GIN BUCK
Juice of ½ Lime and peel
1 drink El Bart Gin
Serve in highball glass with cube of ice and fill up with
Ginger Ale.

GIN SLING
1 piece Domino sugar dissolved in a little water, add a cube
of ice and a drink of Gin. Serve with grated Nutmeg on top.
This can be served hot if desired.

GIN AND TANSY
Place two bunches of tansy in a quart bottle, fill up with
Holland Gin and let stand for about a week. Keep tightly
corked in a cool place. This is excellent as a tonic to improve
the appetite.

HALF AND HALF (American Style)
Fill glass half full of beer and fill up with porter

HALF AND HALF ('ALF AND 'ALF) (English Style)
Fill glass half full of beer and fill up with ale.

HORSE'S NECK
Use Collins glass.
Peel the rind of a lemon in spiral form and place in glass
with one end over the edge, add a cube of ice and fill up
with Ginger Ale.

KNICKERBEIN
Use Port Wine glass.
½ pony Grenadine Syrup
½ pony Maraschino
Yolk of 1 Egg
Top with Brandy

Keep ingredients separate as in a Pousse Cafe.

LONE HEART
Use Cordial glass.

½ pony Maraschino
½ pony Crême Yvette
Top with Cream

MORNING DRINK
Use Hot Water glass.

Juice of ½ Lemon or 2 Limes
Fill up with Hot Water

Float a small spoonful of olive oil on top.

MAMIE TAYLOR
Use Collins glass.

1 drink Scotch Whiskey or Applejack
Juice of 2 Limes
Cube of Ice
Fill up with Ginger Ale

MINT MASH
Use Old Fashioned Cocktail glass.

Muddle 2 pieces Domino Sugar in a little water
½ dozen Mint Leaves
Cube of Ice
1 drink of Rye Whiskey, Bourbon or Gin

Serve with a small spoon.

MERRY WIDOW
Use Sherry glass.

½ Maraschino
½ Cherry Brandy
Decorate with Cherries

MY MARGARET

Use cordial glass.

2/3 Cederlund's Punch
1/3 Brandy
2 dashes Peychaud Bitters

NIGHT CAP

Use Old Fashioned Cocktail glass.
1 teaspoonful Powdered Sugar dissolved in a little water
3 dashes Angostura Bitters
1 drink Holland Gin
Cube of Ice
1 piece of Lemon Peel
1 slice Pineapple
Stir and serve with a small spoon.

OJEN

1 drink Ojen
2 dashes Peychaud Bitters
Shake well in a mixing glass with cracked ice, strain and
serve in a white wine glass.

O'HEARN SPECIAL

Use Collins glass.

Cube of Ice
1 drink * * * Hennessey Brandy
1 piece Orange Peel
2 sprigs fresh Mint
Fill up with Ginger Ale and serve with a spoon.

POMPIER

Use Gobelet.

1 Cube of Ice
1 pony Crême de Cassis
1 drink French Vermouth

Fill up with carbonated water
1 drink * * * Hennessey Brandy

PORT WINE COBBLER

Made same as Sherry Cobbler using Port Wine instead of Sherry.

POUSSE CAFE

Use Cordial glass.

⅙ Grenadine

⅙ Maraschino

⅙ Crême de Menthe (Green)

⅙ Crême de Violette

⅙ Chartreuse (Yellow)

⅙ Brandy

Add in order as given above and keep each cordial separate.

RHINE WINE COBBLER

Made same as Sherry Cobbler using Rhine Wine instead of Sherry.

ROCK AND RYE

Place ¼ lb. rock candy in a quart bottle and fill up with Rye Whiskey. When sugar is dissolved it is ready for use. The bottle should be shaken well each time before serving.

SOUR KISSES

1/3 French Vermouth

2/3 Gin

White of 1 Egg

1 dash Orange Flower Water

Shake well in a mixing glass with cracked ice, strain into a small stem glass and serve.

SANGAREE (SHERRY or PORT)
1 teaspoonful Powdered Sugar
1 drink of liquor desired
Stir well in a mixing glass with cracked ice, strain into a goblet top with a piece of Orange or Lemon peel or a little grated Nutmeg and serve.

SHERRY COBBLER
Use Collins glass.
Fill partly full with finely cracked ice
1 tablespoonful Powdered Sugar
1 drink Sherry Wine
Stir with a spoon until glass is frosted, decorate with fruit and serve with straws.

SHANDY GAFF
Use Collins Glass.
Fill glass half full of Ale and fill up with Ginger Ale.

STINGER
½ White Menthe
½ drink Brandy
Shake well in a mixing glass with cracked ice, strain into large size cocktail glass and serve very cold.

SUISSES
1 jigger White Absinthe
½ jigger Anisette
White of 1 Egg
Shake well in a mixing glass with cracked ice, strain into Fifth Avenue glass and serve.

SWEDISH PUNCH COBBLER
Juice of 2 Limes or 1 Lemon
1 drink Swedish Punch
½ teaspoonful powdered Sugar

Shake well with cracked ice, pour into Collins glass, using more ice if necessary, decorate with fruit and serve with straws.

WALLICK'S MERRY WIDOW
Use Pony glass.

½ Curaçao (white)
½ Cherry Brandy

Note delicious flavor.

WARD'S
Use large Cocktail glass.

½ pony Chartreuse
½ pony Brandy
1 piece Orange

Arrange Orange peel in bottom of glass to form a circle, fill up with finely cracked ice, add the Chartreuse and Brandy and decorate with fresh mint.

Different cordials can be used if desired.

WILD EYED ROSE
Juice ½ Lime
½ pony Grenadine
1 drink of Irish Whiskey

Serve in highball glass with cube of ice and fizz with carbonated water.

WILSON DISTILLING COMPANY SPECIAL
1 drink El Bart Gin
2 dashes French Vermouth
2 slices Blood Orange
Shake well in a mixing glass with cracked ice, strain into Whiskey glass and serve.

WITCHING EYE
Use Cordial glass.

2/3 Crême de Cacao
Top with Cream
1 dash Angostura Bitters

YOU NEVER KNOW
Use bar glass.

1 drink Blackberry Brandy
3 dashes Nutmeg
2 dashes Essence of Peppermint

Printed in Great Britain
by Amazon